To order additional copies of this book, contact:
Xlibris
1-888-795-4274
www.Xlibris.com
Orders@Xlibris.com

ISBN: Softcover   978-1-4836-1418-2
       Hardcover   978-1-4836-5661-8
       EBook   978-1-4836-1419-9

Library of Congress Control Number: 2013905267

Print information available on the last page

Rev. date: 10/10/2019

DEDICATION

This book is dedicated to Alprett Young (my sister), Princess Wallace (my daughter), Woodrow Wallace III   (my son), and those who seek peace, harmony, along with everlasting life instead of death.   My sister, my daughter, and my son I hold dearest to my heart; therefore, I dedicate Verses to you.

WELCOME TO FOREVER! ENJOY!!!

ACKNOWLEDGEMENTS

I thank God for the knowledge of the coming of the Kingdom of God. I thank God for Jesus, the Son, Who performed the great sacrifice.

PREFACE

Often times, information is made available to an individual and more than not, opportunity for growth passes one bye; however, perpetual opportunity for growth exist and one will find doors of opportunity continually opening in Verses.

I grew up in a poor neighborhood but the community was rich with love for one another, which provided tremendous opportunity to engage, communicate, and share ideas. I was fortunate to have grown up around individuals who possessed multiple opinions, outlooks, and beliefs on issues pertaining to Mankind, God, and spiritual growth.

Verses will share with the reader poems of diversity, which contain an avenue to spiritual growth. Spiritual growth is not finite; therefore, the message reflects simplicity but is powerfully huge to digest in the state of carnal mindedness.

The message in Verses clearly gives rise to inner examination, self-awareness, and opportunity to engage spiritual growth. The inner workings of man are complex and none singular in nature; therefore, man's complexity is at odds with himself. The man who has not experienced his own complexities is frighteningly numb to me.

One's complexities consist of the consciousness to know, feel, and interact with the carnal-physical and spiritual-inner self. Interacting and living harmoniously is not the same; for, one has to be mindful of one's own differences to appreciate fully the opposite roles the carnal-physical and spiritual-inner self dictate.

The spiritual body and the physical body are not in synchronization, which can present stagnation in an individual; ultimately, one must work at sinequanon growth toward God to acquire and maintain spiritual growth. One must seek absolute faith, hope, and charity to contend for eternal life. Make no mistake in judgment, for we are contending because the battle is with the carnal-physical self, which wants to please the body, while the spiritual-inner self wants to please God.

Verses presents to the reader the challenge to research, verify, and apply the compacted poetic information, which the author firmly attests will assist anyone who seeks spiritual growth. Verses reveal a poetic message of splendor unequalled in approach to spiritual growth through intellect and simplicity for the enhancement of modern day poetry. Verses are a vagary in the world of modern day poetry.

Verses are a one of a kind read, which introduces a new style of writing from Woodrow Wallace. Verses offer solace, direction, and hope in times of joy and despair. Verses are a collection of poems accentuating an absolute volume of meaning within each line, stanza, and page, which exposes its uniqueness.

Woodrow Wallace introduces to the reader the surround reading style (SRS). SRS is a style of poetry that captures and holds the theme, message, and inspirational outcome from every angle of the poem; even, when read in reverse (top to bottom) or (bottom to top), the message remains the same. Welcome, to SRS poetry, Verses, by Woodrow Wallace

VERSES

How to Interpret and Understand This Book

By

Woodrow Wallace

To reap the rewards Verses provides one must embrace Verses as a spiritual, poetic, and educational book that offers life changing experiences when applied diligently. Verses is designed to reward the reader by unlocking the poetic message within each poem through the follow-up biblical scripture of affirmation found in the biblical passages, which clarify, reinforce, and strengthen one's ability to change carnal behaviors that conflict with spiritual growth.

Man often reflects on his past for guidance, struggles to survive in the present, and tries to plan his future; therefore, man is barely savoring his present state of being. Hindsight is 20/20; therefore, what is-done, is seldom undone, without repercussions, while planning the future entails many adjustments.

By design, Verses is a book of poetry that gives the reader more than an eventful read because the message makes sense of the past while giving the reader spiritual enlightenment, which perpetually creates a present environment conducive to obtaining spiritual growth and eternal life. Verses is a poetic revelation and tool created to give the reader a simple approach to understanding man's carnal-physical and spiritual-inner environments, while transforming the individual from carnal mortality to spiritual immortality.

Verses unveils a mirror that reflects one's past, shows one's present, and opens a portal to one's spiritual future, while facilitating ways to deal with a world that focuses on carnal-physical self.

As in life there is no short cuts; therefore, each poem must-be-read first to get the author's message of simplicity associated to events that enhance or hinder spiritual growth; afterwards, one has-to-read the entire suggested biblical chapter. Focus on the emphasized verses and compare the researched biblical scriptures for conformational purposes, which attest, reinforce, and magnify the poetic message. The knowledge and wisdom one may obtain from Verses is tantamount to spiritual salience; however, the information is not intricate, rather intrinsically God like. Man's existence is mammoth, which validates man as the number one momentous candidate for God-like everlasting life, because man's spiritual-inner self is infinite, which surpasses mere chance.

CONTENTS

"SOME ADVISE"

Slander not today or tomorrow
Lest you bring forth your sorrow;
Be not boastful, colorful, or loud
Lest you walk arrogant and proud

Sanction not the fool's word
Lest your life becomes absurd;
Seek not the bully's ways
Lest your children have shorter days.

Slow yourself to vain speech
Lest you fall to Satan's reach;
Abstain from the drunkard life
Lest you inherit a world of sigh.

Depart from anger in your youth
Seek the Word and the truth;
No one knows their appointed end
For, death is the price for sin.

Proverbs – (Chapter 3) Emphasis: Verses 3, 11, 12, 13, 14, 15, 16, 17, 18

"A GAMBLER"

A Gambler-
Is co-signer to a stranger's fortune?
Surely the sun will rise;
Because a Gambler's
Treasures will set in the stranger's coffer.

A Gambler-
Who chooses to marry?
Surely will meet with loss;
Because a Gambler's
Power is nothing in the game of chance.

A Gambler-
Wages tangible and intangible assets
Surely, the loss is greater than money;
Because a Gambler's
Knowledge of longevity is lacking.

A Gambler-
Feels deeper pains than a drunkard
Surely, the pain is perpetual;
Because a Gambler's
Losses comes often times when sober.

How do I know?
I was a Gambler.

Proverbs – (Chapter 11) Emphasis: Verses 4, 28, 29

"ECHO"

Have you heard about this and that?
Will you pray or lay a bet?
From BC to AD, came awfully fast
Moments-of-truth, appear atlas.

"Trust in me," Man's old cliché
Remember the Serpent and Eve's day?
Gather your armor, make your stand
Is it for oil, or your fellow Man?

Many do war in God's Holy Names
Selfish fools play fleshly games;
Futile attempts will always be made
However, the path for Man has been laid.

Even Love cries for a clone
No Love exists to be alone;
Out of deliverance, comes some sanity
Even in this, all is vanity.

Proverbs – (Chapter 1) Emphasis: Verses 20, 21, 22, 28, 29, 30, 31, 32, 33

"THE HONDURAN"

Like Nebuchadnezzar's madness-
Time befalls all Men
Even in FCI Fort Dix, you can find a friend;
Like Daniel in the lion's den-
Blackie spoke to me today
A compassionate fellow I must say.

Like a bag of dry bones-
He works the line wrapping plastic silverware
Thinking of home with sadness and care
Like the interpretation of a dream-
He awaits Immigration's mighty call
To deliver him from his hellish fall.

Like healing waters-
He recounts his times back home
Wishing for the sea, how long, how long?
Like distant borders-
He anticipates his release
A family reunion and a big ole-feast.

Like a prophecy-
Blackie's life does unfold
Revealing a man with a soul;
Like the reunion of Judah and Israel-
He shall return to family and his land
Moreover, God shall cradle him in his hand.

"WARNING"

In the day of the Storm!
The Wind shall be like Jehu-
The mighty works of Man shall fall
Similar to the House of Ahab.
The basket awaits the head of Man,
Like unto the letters sent to Samaria
The Good-News is sent to Man
For the Kingdom of God is at hand!

2 Kings – (Chapter 9) Emphasis: Verses 24, 25
2 Kings – (Chapter 10) Emphasis: Verses 8, 9, 10, 11

"A Moment of Truth"

To know, perceive, and understand
Is wealth and treasure in thy hand?
A Proverb gives wise instruction
To offset Man's self-destruction.

Young Men give hope to the world
Likewise, the birth, of a girl;
Beware, little Girl and Boy
Refrain from the sinful toy.

The righteous, sometimes lose their way
Then, sorrow and travail, has its say;
So, fight the good fight, do not quit
For, only darkness lies in the pit.

To accept the gift of eternal life
Is like unto a fool's lasting strife;
If Wisdom called, out to you?
Tell me now, what would you do?

Proverbs – (Chapter 2) Emphasis: Verses 3, 4, 5
Proverbs – (Chapter 3) Emphasis: Verses 11, 12, 13, 14, 15, 16

"LOOKING OUT THE WINDOW

Man is perpetual in his sinful way
A thousand years are like unto a day;
He labors on without Godly fear
While end of days, draws decisively near.

In due time penalty comes to be
Eyes wide-shut, Man cannot see;
The lost generations, lingers behind
For the Good-News, few shall find.

The author of confusion always deceive
The Sons of Man refuse to believe;
A new beginning, One has made
The debt for sin has been paid.

Ears of the young, continue to die
While faces of the old, sag and cry
Voices of understanding quash temptation.
Moreover, doers of deceit will miss salvation.

Proverbs – (Chapter 6) Emphasis: Verses 16, 17, 18, 19
Proverbs – (Chapter 6) Emphasis: Verses 6, 7, 8, 9

"Listen Up"

Pains of truth cut deeper than steel
Wrath of God I favor none to feel:
Fools contract with the deceiver
Likewise, the gambler and unbeliever.

Highways of life twist and turn
Governors of deceit surely will burn;
Double standards are easy to portray
Judas and Jesus remember that day.

Know the truth, prepare thy-self
Real fear lies, in the second death;
Merry of heart often masks the truth
Search the Word discover the proof.

Who is perfect that falls short of glory?
Take some time and read the story;
Life boils down to the Master's Plan
Which was conceived before earth and Man.?

Proverbs – (Chapter 18) Emphasis: Verses 6, 7, 8, 21
Proverbs – (Chapter 14) Emphasis: Verse 12

"WISDOM AND UNDERSTANDING"

Why wander or guess at the truth?
Look around, witness the proof;
Does anyone stop, think, or care?
From the beginning, two were there.

They called out to the Sons of Man
To provide Man a helping hand;
Unlike darkness Wisdom heals
The secret things, Understanding reveals.

There is no likeness of the two
They knew the earth before me and you;
They are there at God's beckoning call
Wisdom and Understanding created it all.

Always standing tall and strong
Ushering in truth and devouring all wrong;
Receive them and set yourself free
I once was blind but now I see (The Holy Bible, 2009).

Proverbs – (Chapter 8) Emphasis: Verses 22, 35, 36
1Corinthians – (Chapter 2) Emphasis: Verses 6, 7, 8, 9
John – (chapter 9) Emphasis; Verses 24, 25, 31, 32, 33, 39

"IN THE DAY OF MAN"

In subtle things the battle rages
familiar grounds same old cages;
Like unto soldiers at war forever
The life of Man is that endeavor.

Enemies stab at Man's naked back
However, truth covers Man, that is a fact;
Protection is always at Man's side
John 3:16 whom shall hide?

The battle is fought for me and you
Make no mistake these words are true;
Charge was given to the Son of Nun
Likewise, do not, turn and run.

Be of good cheer my sister and brother
The covenant binds us one to another;
As life withers from the roses
We shall sing the Song of Moses.

2Timothy – (Chapter 2) Emphasis: Verses 2, 3, 4,
Deuteronomy – (Chapter 31) Emphasis: Verse 23
Deuteronomy – Chapter 32) Emphasis: Verses All

"PROVERBS 23:9"

I want be passing this way again
Remember this, my solemn friend;
The promise remains the same
The struggle is not a childish game.

Did opportunity pass you by?
Do you embrace the same ole-lie?
Wish and hope for something new?
Who can make your grey sky blue?

An encouraging word I have instead
Seek the truth, depart from the dead;
Quench your thirst, live forever
The Master's plan is truly clever.

What will you do for salvation today?
Fold your arms continue to play?
Loose thy-self from the scorpion's sting
Through Solomon, seek the principal thing

Proverbs – (Chapter 23) Emphasis: Verse 9
John – (Chapter 14) Emphasis: Verses 1
Proverbs – (Chapter 4) Emphasis: Verse 7

"LOVE"

If charity is found in your youth?
You have a life full of truth;
Charity is always on point and call
Charity is diversified in us all.

Charity labors not in carnal feeling
Charity answers not, I'm just chill' in;
Charity knows Man sees only in part
Charity is rare in a cold-dark heart.

Charity completes Man with all truth
1Corinthians 13:2 is living proof;
Perfection will eventually come to Man
When Charity blankets all the land.

Man's sweet reward of pure love
The Revelation comes from above;
The message comes in triple clarity
The greatest, has always been charity.

1Corinthians - (Chapter 13) Emphasis: Verses 2, 9, 10, 13

"Spiritual Awareness"

Solitude was never meant for Man
The collective body was the plan;
Living amongst millions but alone
Like the sinner, without a home.

Fear of fellowship, stagnates us all
Giving rise, to Satan's call;
Groups are stronger than mere one
Even multiple bullets are in a gun.

A caring community is the key
Loving each other sets us free;
This is what really matters most
The Father, Son, and Holy Ghost.

Mercy and forgiveness renews the soul
Search your heart, meet the goal;
Forgiving each other, we must do
Who forgave more, than God for you?

Ephesians – (Chapter 4) Emphasis: Verse 32

"REFLECTIONS"

Sometimes we have good days
No pain, no hurt, no betrays;
Count your blessing, my good friend
Tomorrow starts all over again.

What will be, has always been
A new beginning, an old end;
The death of Man is true life
Man fights, prolonging his strife.

More knowledge, more pain
Man rides, the run-away-train;
Man knows, he cannot stay
Despite all, Man fights anyway.

Man's story deeply saddens me
Because it did not have to be;
Come, see, what Man has done
Man cannot charge-off this one.

John – (chapter 8) Emphasis: Verse 8
John – (Chapter 8) Emphasis: Verses 43, 44, 45, 46, 47

"Message from the Past"

You who live now, curse not life
Seek not death prepare for strife;
Hold your memories, deep within yourself
Spoil no ears, put talk on the shelf.

Know this, as One tells you
Trust not this world, its untrue;
Keep high spirits, be strong today
Tomorrow promises not another stay.

All your plans, do they exist?
Only One holds, the eternal fix;
Never mind your wants and desires
Likely, they lead to hellish fires.

Be it love for a woman or man
Include the One in that plan;
For family, friend, and associate be glad
Surely, the day cometh that is very sad.

The older we get, luck runs short
One sacrificed, our lives were bought;
Just when we think, it is a win
Life shows up all over my friend!

Ecclesiastes – (Chapter 5) Emphasis: Verses 2, 3, 6, 7
      (Chapter 2) Emphasis: Verses 2, 9, 10, 11, 22, 23, 24, 25, 26
John – (Chapter 2) Emphasis: Verses 15, 16, 17

"AN AH HA MOMENT"

(Solomon)

Listen my friend, this is a story
About inequality, vanity, wisdom, and glory
Is anything new under the sun?
A generation passes and another comes.

Solomon, the wisest, you will ever know
Dedicated his life, to learn even more;
He searched everything, up and down
Only to confirm, no end is found.

Solomon amassed the best of everything
There was nothing, Solomon did not redeem;
Having all of this, Solomon was not free
Only vexation of spirit was Solomon's discovery.

Solomon, the wisest, wallowed in sorrow
Because nothing changes, not even
tomorrow;
Solomon's heart was filled with despair
For Solomon's labors fall to another's care.

A time for everything, Solomon surely
found
A time to live, a time to clown;
For good men die, doing righteous things
While bad men live and wickedness they
bring.

What Happens to one, happens to all
We are born of sin, and then we fall;
No, matter your estate, my friend
The same to all, death in the end.

Solomon says this, to me and you
Love God and thy neighbor too;
For every secret thing come to light
Whether it is wrong or it is right.

Ecclesiastes – (Chapter 1) Emphasis: Verses 3, 4
 (Chapter 7) Emphasis; Verse 14
 (Chapter 3) Emphasis: Verses 1, 15
 (Chapter 11) Emphasis: Verses
 7, 8, 9, 10
 (Chapter 12) Emphasis:
 Verses 12, 13, 14

"The Miracle on the Road to Damascus"

One never knows what maybe
One like Saul, who persecuted thee;
Once the jailer, now the salvation
God often changes, Man's life and station.

God saw to change Saul's ways
Gave Saul Ananias, lengthening his days;
A burning bush, the Damascus stroll
Revealed the commitment on Saul's soul.

Persecutor of Christians is now dead
New man arises, called Paul instead;
Moreover, Paul's recompense is without guiles
Paul's calling is to all the Gentiles.

Jerusalem to Rome and back again
Paul is arrested, preaching against sin;
Howbeit the Jews long-suffering grow.
Christ is silenced? Do not they know?

When Christ came, none gave praise
Thus, ushered in shortness of days;
Without three principals lies only disparity
Paul taught number one is always charity.

Acts – (Chapter 9) Emphasis: Verses 3, 4, 5, 6   (Chapter 13) Emphasis: Verses 9, 10, 11, 12
(Chapter 22) Emphasis: Verses 6, 7, 8, 9, 10, 11, 12, 13, 14, 15, 16

"JUST A REMINDER"

Jesus returned to Jerusalem on a beautiful day
To fulfill the true prophecy in a new way;
Remember the one who did betray
The Light of the world with a sop that day.

The mystery was cloaked when the journey began
For only God knew the true heart of Man;
Be not dismayed for Moses did foretell
Discover salvation or risk burning in hell.

John – (chapter 12) Emphasis: Verses 12, 13, 14, 15, 16
      (Chapter 13) Emphasis: Verses 21, 22, 25, 26, 27
Mathews – (Chapter 21) Emphasis: Verses 4, 5, 6, 9
      (Chapter 26) Emphasis: Verses 48, 49

Printed in the United States
By Bookmasters